What Successf
Say Abou
Trench Marketing

"Rudy's simple, three-step process crosses all languages, ages, education and industries, insuring success for all who are disciplined and committed. In addition to Piccolo, I have four different retail businesses that grew from day one after we rolled out *Marketing from the Trenches*. This book is a priceless addition to any training program."

Tom Valenti, Proprietor
Piccolo Ristorante, New York

❖ ❖ ❖

"Rudy's marketing program is brilliant. His presentation is packed with energy and style, drive and determination. He keeps you interested and you leave believing you can slay giants. The only thing better than attending his program was measuring the results! Outstanding!"

Steve Ogden, Former Five-Unit Owner
West Coast Video, Pennsylvania

"One of the biggest challenges in running a successful Martial Arts school is balancing tradition and business. Rudy's *Marketing from the Trenches* keeps me right on track."

Sensei Pedro Ramirez, Proprietor
TUF Academy of Martial Arts, Georgia

❖ ❖ ❖

"I rolled out Rudy's program after attending his seminar, and it has become instrumental to the daily success of our marketing efforts. Increasing interaction with customers and establishing business partnerships in our trade areas have been two of the most effective strategies we've applied to enhance our presence.

The results are clear and measurable: increased traffic and sales. *Marketing from the Trenches* is a smart, low-cost method that will steer your business in the right direction and deliver extraordinary results."

Mark McNall, Division Vice President
ACE Cash Express, Inc., Texas

"This exceptional marketing guide is packed with effective, easy-to-implement strategies guaranteed to grow any business. Rudy's common-sense approach, cultivated through hands-on experience in many retail industries, should be widely adopted as standard practice in today's small and commercial business models."

Jaime De La Vega,
Former Operations Manager
Avis Car Rentals, New York/Florida

❖❖❖

"Waldner's deceptively simple approach to complex marketing strategies has played an invaluable role in increasing our sales and customer service. Inspirational, engaging and motivating, *Marketing from the Trenches* is required reading for all business owners. Highly recommended!"

Peter Blake, Curator
Peter Blake Gallery, California

"Waldner weaves anecdotes and action plans into a concise strategy for revenue growth. He provides a playbook of behavioral tactics that are both measurable and designed to enhance customer generation. A must read for family business managers, multi-unit managers, first-time managers, and budding entrepreneurs."

Darren C. Treadway, Ph.D.,
Assistant Professor of Management
University of Mississippi

Marketing
from the
Trenches
Your Guide to Retail Success

How to grow your business from
behind your counter

Rudolf J. Waldner

Gotham City
PUBLISHERS

Marketing from the Trenches
Copyright 2006 by Rudolf J. Waldner

Gotham City Publishers, Atlanta, GA
TrenchMarketer@aol.com
www.TrenchMarketer.com
www.Facebook.com/TrenchMarketer

10-Digit ISBN: 0-9789893-0-9
13-Digit ISBN: 978-0-9789893-0-9
Library of Congress Control Number: 2006938246
Copyright: TXul-319-179

Cover and art work: Manjari Graphics
Cartoons: Al De La Vega
Layout: J. L. Saloff
Fonts: GarmondPro, URW Alcuin, Worstveld Sting

Second Edition

*Printed in the United States of America
on acid free paper.*

For all who do the right thing,
All the time,
No matter what.

Keep Believing. . .

Contents

Acknowledgments
&
Thank Yous

Acknowledgments & Thank Yous

First and foremost, I need to thank all of the people who embraced the Trench Marketing concept, grew their businesses, and helped me prove that the program works—*if you work the program.*

A great big thank you to Debi G, who believed in me and the program, even though we were surrounded by quite an obstinate group of "Nay-Sayers."

To Oliver on the West Coast, who kept urging me to put the program into book form, thank you.

To writer, editor, and close personal friend since grade school, Claire Curry, who's been there every step of the way. Thank you, I could not have done it without you—truly.

To Jefrey Taylor, musician, performer, song writer, and best of friends, thank you for adding focus. "A different labyrinth, but the same unicorn."

I'd also like to express my gratitude to Jay Conrad Levinson and his *Guerilla Marketing* series. His works confirmed that I was headed in the right direction.

And finally, to my loving companion, who looks up at me with wholehearted support no matter what I choose to do, just for a scratch on her belly and a chance to lick my face: my mini-Dachshund, Strudl.

Inspirations

I remember working in a car wash, one of two jobs at the time, putting myself through college. I was wearing orange overalls and soaked with sweat. My next gig was a rather messy large yellow car that had never even seen a vacuum cleaner.

I got into the task wholeheartedly. One half-hour later I came up for air and had transformed the car into a respectable automobile. The car owner's smile was enormous. It was as if the afternoon's sunshine was reflecting off of his bright, white teeth. I remember that smile vividly and think of it often, whenever I lose sight of why I do what I do. It's all about that smile. It's all about a happy customer.

While managing my family deli—my introduction to the world of business—there was no better way to get a New Yorker to smile than to save him time with fast, quality service. Before a regular customer walked through my front door, their coffee was poured and ready to go. Black with two sugars, that's how my first customer of the day took his. Always at 5:59 a.m. Talk about a smile! Probably the first and last smile he'd share until the end of his commute.

I can go on with anecdotes and real-life experiences that have taught me important lessons about business and have kept me motivated through many hours of hard work in various jobs, but I won't. I'll just summarize. What inspired me and influenced the creation of my marketing program was literally working *in the trenches*, behind the counter in many different industries. Steaming a cappuccino, stirring a martini, delivering a pizza, creating a dinner menu, merchandising a video rental wall, preparing client taxes, underwriting a loan, running a booth at an industrial trade show, soliciting institutional investors by phone, and so on. What I learned is this: success in every business is anchored by only one thing—a happy customer.

Introduction

Hi there. **My name is Rudy.** I've worked in retail, marketing, and sales management for my entire professional career. Without fail, I've taken multi-unit and single-unit businesses to documented new highs in revenue and customer count.

I'm here to share with you my simple Trench Marketing Program. It's really a mindset that will make it possible to grow your business significantly, without paying huge dollars for hard-to-qualify (or justify) advertising.

In the following pages, I'll walk you through the three simple steps of my program and I guarantee that if you implement the tools you'll learn throughout these pages, you'll become even more successful than you already are. So strap on your seat belts as I blow what's left of your conditioned mind, and open up a huge new world of self-contained and self-sufficient growth strategies.

Something's Gotta Give

How it All Began

I'm preparing for a date. My heart is racing with all out "woo-hoo" anticipation.

As I begin to prepare my place for the event—cleaning, freshening, hiding stuff, etc.— I have MTV on the screen. I like and almost need music blaring to kick the adrenalin into high gear, as cleaning doesn't excite me.

Thirty minutes later, as I walk out the door to pick up wine and some other delicacies, I realize there wasn't any music on TV but some reality show dribble and *commercials*—all of which I had blocked out for the full 30 minutes.

I jump into my Jeep, turn the radio volume up to neighbor-annoying-level, only to realize that there's a *radio commercial* blaring, not sure for what, because I shut it off. Down the road, I pass a very cool *billboard* for something I promised myself I'd remember, but forgot. A few minutes later, I arrive at the supermarket; by the way, don't tell anyone that I buy my wine there. Only after I vault out of the Jeep do I realize that I had ridden in silence. (OK, maybe I hummed {yelled} a few bars {the whole thing} of Green Day's "Basket Case," but nobody needs to know that either.)

I trot to the wine aisle and grab a bottle each of red, white, and dessert wine. (Keeping all my options open, if you're with me.) So I have one bottle in each hand, the third under my arm. I'm heading for the fresh-cut flowers when I reach for a *newspaper insert* filled with coupons. I thumb through en route. With my head in the paper, balancing the bottles, I bump into a *shelf-talker*. (You've no doubt seen many of these, but if your unfamiliar with its official name, a shelf-talker is one of those handy little gadgets attached to the lip of a shelf – some vomit coupons or even light up – designed to draw your attention to a promoted product.) As I jerk up and step back, I drop one of the wine bottles. It smashes to the floor loudly, creating a very sad, wonderfully aromatic puddle of Pinotage—my favorite, by the way. Under the quickly forming red stain, right on the tiles, there's a *floor decal* for tile cleaner. Funny, I thought, and ironic.

I'm blocking the aisle as I try and push the glass shards to the side with my shoe. A senior drives her kart into my backside (better than into my Jeep, right?) as I'm adjusting the two remaining bottles into a firmer grip. I peel myself from her kart's grill and notice a message on the *kart-talker* that says, "Learn to Drive, call 1-800-blah, blah, blah." (Another nifty gadget. A "kart-talker" is a fancy name for an advertising sign mounted on to a shopping kart.)

Just stop! I can't take it anymore. Too many messages...too much input. With so much unsolicited information assaulting me at once, I'm not able to see or hear anything! Instead, I am blocking out all the "noise" and these expensive, crafty advertising tactics are falling on deaf ears. There's got to be a better way!

I digress. Back to Aisle 11 with the red puddle and kart-talker...

I slap my forehead, saying to myself, **ENOUGH!** But of course, it isn't over yet. The slapping motion tilts my head up slightly and my eyes bulge in disbelief— skateboarding into the *ceiling tile* is a pair of cardboard sneakers and a cardboard street kid's arm holding a soft drink. As I continue to stare heavenwards, utterly dumbfounded, the *supermarket speaker system* drones, "Cleanup in Aisle 11," interrupting a perfectly good *in-house ad* for... %$#@!

Advertisers have an official term for this chaos: it's called clutter. And they'd like you to believe that buying *more* ad space is the answer to breaking through the clutter and capturing consumer attention and dollars. Not for my money.

Can you feel my frustration? Probably the same as yours. We're all drowning in ads, can't hear ourselves think, and the only solution that advertisers offer is to buy more ad space, which just creates more clutter, and so on, and so on...

Something's gotta give! Read on, there IS a better way.

The Opportunity:

Cold Hard Facts

Here's the issue. The United States houses about 4% of the world's population, yet we're flooded with nearly 70% of the world's mass media. No wonder thousands of advertising dollars fall on deaf ears.

According to author and marketer Seth Godin in his fantastic book *Permission Marketing*, a 10% recall rate from a TV ad campaign is considered a success. That means that if one out of 10 people even *remember* your ad, the industry considers it a success. Just to point out the obvious, "recall rate" does *not* equal sales. Furthermore, rates keep climbing and ratings keep plummeting. Ratings are going down because the TV market is getting fragmented. Fragmented means more stations and choices, therefore less viewers available per station.

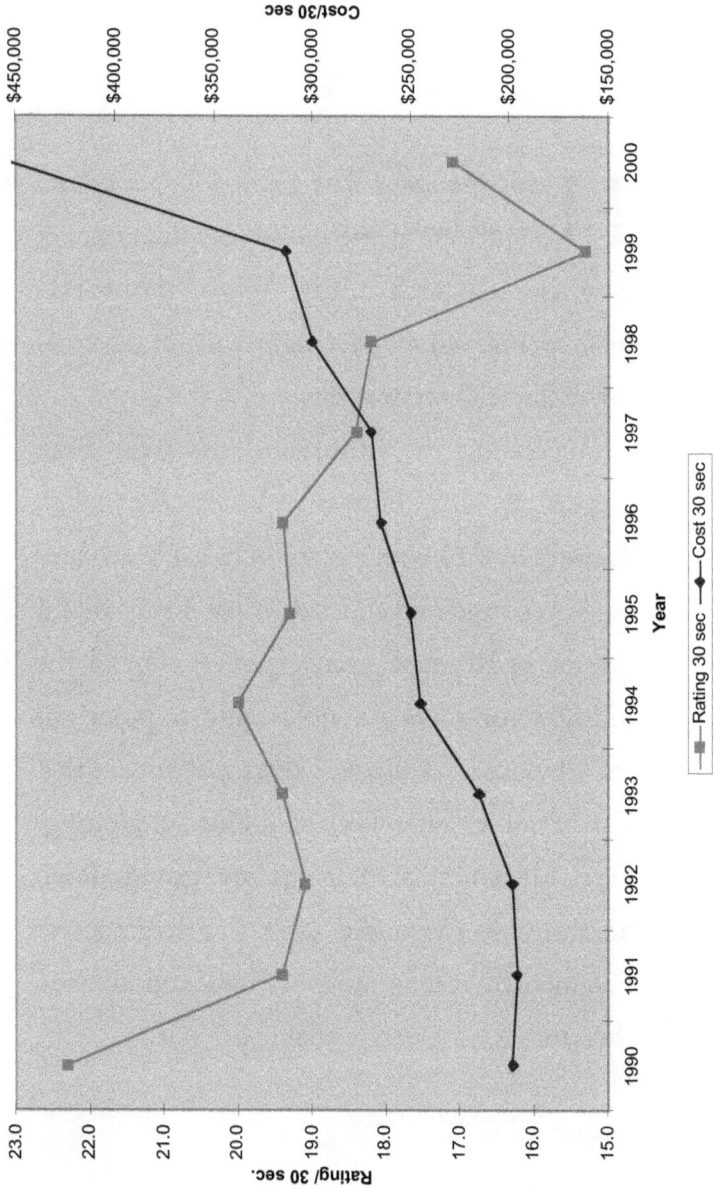

Cost per 30 Second TV Spot

Here's some hard data to prove my point. The graph at the left overlays the decrease in ratings with the increase of the cost for a 30-second TV spot for the last decade of the 20th century.

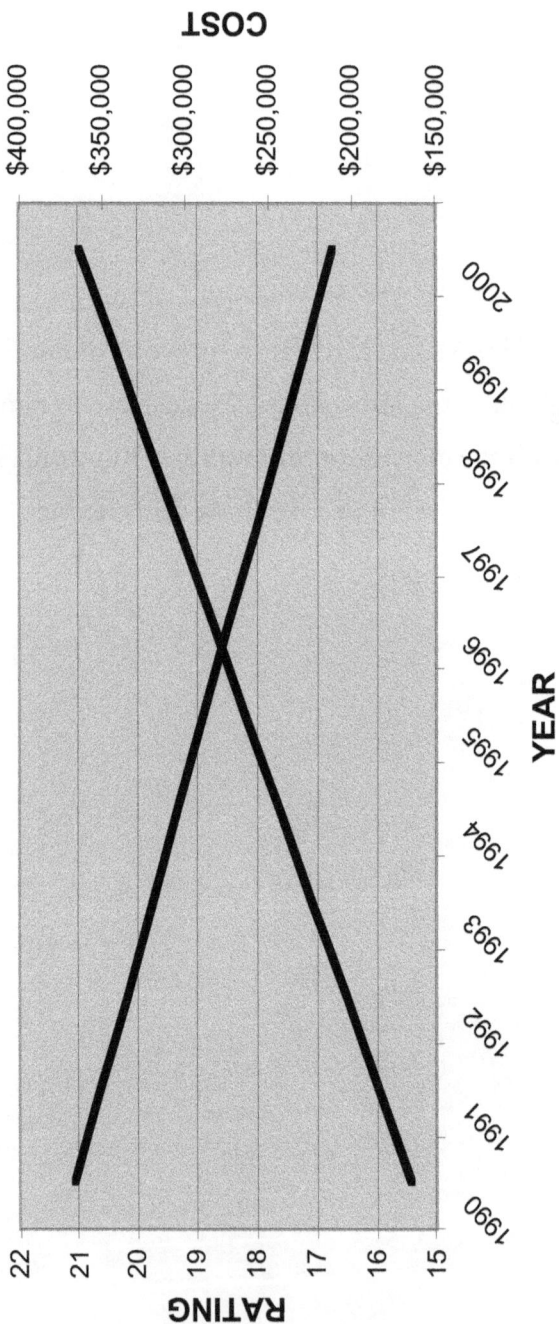

COST PER 30s TV SPOT

The graph at the left smoothes the results, creating a solid trend line. (The textbook definition of smoothing a graph is to "free it from irregularities by ignoring random variations.")

I can't make it any more clear: ratings continue to plummet, costs per spot soar, cost-per-customer acquisition is the highest versus any other type of marketing, and the entire end result is measured by a "recall rate," not even by sales or new customer count.

Direct Mail is another one of my favorites. Here, a one-percent response rate is deemed a huge success. But let me translate: if you send out 100 mailers and generate ONE customer, that's considered a success. Yes, you read that right. Me, I'm a bit more practical-minded. My take is that that these results represent, literally, a 99% *failure* rate. I prefer to spend my money (wisely) on proven strategies that deliver concrete, measurable results. I'll share them with you soon, but first let's wrap up the facts. Read on.

"Recall rate" is one industry indicator used by advertising agencies to measure success. Another is "cost-per-customer acquisition." How much does it cost to drive a customer through your door? Based on current research, to acquire a customer from a TV ad, advertising can cost anywhere from $85 to $95 per customer. The cost-per-customer acquisition for direct mail hovers around $45 to $55. That said, I've just reviewed another study that tallies the cost-per-customer acquisition for a combination radio and direct mail campaign at over $1,000 per new customer. These numbers are all over the place, depending on who is pitching what. But roughly speaking, they offer a point of comparison for the program outlined in this book which has, time after time, driven results to the very digestible tune of $10 to $25 cost-per-customer acquisition. Now we're talking, right?

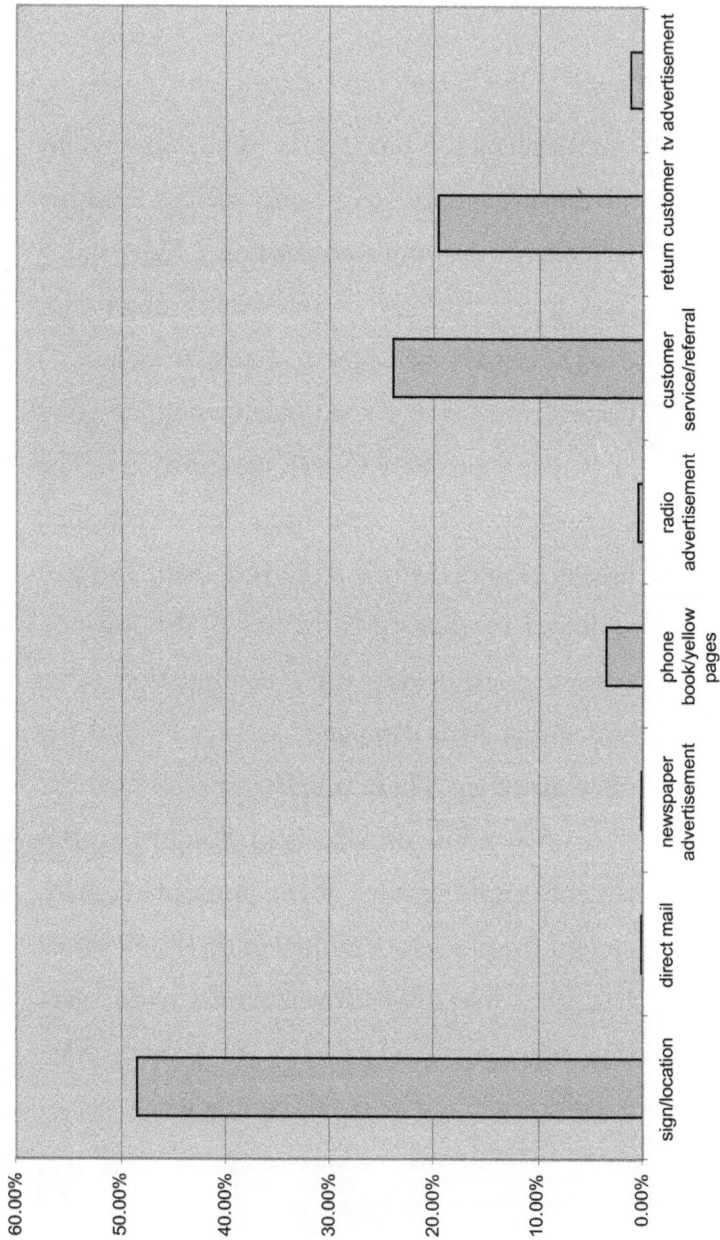

Detailed Source Analysis

One more graph to underscore the point yet again, ad nauseam. These are the results from a company that spent thousands of dollars on advertising. All customers were asked, "How'd you hear about us?" Now take a moment to really absorb these results:

The graph at the left shows that 1.81% of new customers came from Radio, TV, Newspaper, and Direct Mail. (.02 + .18 + .52 + 1.09 = 1.81) What's more important though is the other 92%. **All of these new customers were not driven to this company's doors through costly methods of advertising, but rather simple strategies that are within every business owner's direct control!**

Signs	48.46%
Referrals	24.03%
Return Customers	<u>19.60%</u>
	92.09%

Customer service and location drive 90+% of your business. That's the fact. **So the point is, it really is all about you.**

In case your not a millionaire yet, or you're tired of ineffective and unqualified advertising dollars hitting your P&L, get ready to embrace a clear and concise methodology for growing your business. Oh yeah, it's fun, too.

(Remember, if you're not having fun in whatever it is you are doing, you shouldn't be doing it.)

A Story of Success

So without further delay, let's jump right in. Rather recently, I was an operations and marketing executive managing over 150 retail units spanning many states. I'd identified an underperforming, isolated store in a fairly rural town on the West Coast. Just looking at the results on paper, you would probably board the place up and cut your losses. Curious, I decided to fly out and take a look at the location. Middle management was along for the ride, claiming they'd had problems with the previous staff.

Before the trip and under my directive, the staff had been "upgraded." The new players were poised to buy into my Trench Marketing Program. When I walked in, the location was spotless. I was approached and greeted by a smiling employee who made eye contact and shook my hand confidently. So far, so good. The glass and counters sparkled, evidence of a sense of pride and ownership. Even better. I had the employee role-play a few customer service exercises. Again, perfect and drenched with enthusiasm. She handed me a coupon of great value that she'd gotten from a business partner to share with all of her customers. It doesn't get better than this.

Lesson: Keep your place spotless, staff with energetic people who WANT to be there, and form business partnerships within your trade area. That's all it takes, every hour of every day that you're open for business.

Following are some statistics reflecting the impact of the program at this location:

June: Staff "upgraded"
Mid July: 21% increase in customer base
End of July: bad debt improved by 60%

These are actual results from a location that dragged down the P&L of an entire division for over two years. After we rolled out the program, *voilà*, the results speak for themselves!

Trench Marketing Defined

Before I dig in, let's tackle conventional marketing once and for all. Grab a blue pen and thick black marker for this exercise. I'll wait, I promise. OK, here we go.

As defined by most reference books:

> *"Marketing is the systematic planning, implementation, and control of a mix of business activities intended to bring together buyers and sellers for mutually advantageous exchange or transfer of products."*

(Try and keep your food down.) Do you think the scribe who developed this definition ever emerged from behind his desk and interacted with a real, live customer?

Now for the good part, and kind of my way of saying *sorry* for making you read the above "definition." Cross it out with the thick marker. Go ahead. **DO IT!**

Now pick up the pen and on the following lines, write the following sentence, word for word.

"Trench Marketing is
everything that I can do to
grow my own business."

And then underline the word **I**.

_____

_____

_____

_____

_____

Does that feel like ownership? Good, because it is. If you believe this with every breath you take, you will be an overwhelming success. Now you're ready. Here we go.

Next page please. . .

The Three "P"s: Place, People, Partners

Everything
related to
success
demands
action

It's time to examine the three "P"s—the three steps to Trench Marketing success. I'll call them **action steps**, as everything related to success demands *action*.

PLACE

Action Step I. The first "P" stands for PLACE. This means doing everything possible to control the atmosphere and ambiance of your work place. Feed all the senses, all the time, with something wonderful, or at least positive. Here's how.

Feed all the
senses,
all the time,
with something
wonderful,
or at least
positive

Sight. *What the customer sees.* Aside from aesthetics, themes, and motifs—all of which are important—cleanliness is key. Every surface must be spotless, always. I once saw a beautiful gold embossed painting from Thailand in a small restaurant that had cobwebs between it and the wall it hung on. Yuck! I wouldn't want to spend a dollar of my hard-earned money at that place.

The first thing a customer or potential customer sees—whatever your product is—is your front door and the sidewalk and parking lot leading to it. Remember this basic principle: *cleanliness = credibility.*

Remember
this basic
principle:

cleanliness = credibility

I ran a small group of stores for a national video chain. The division consisted of a handful of video rental stores in New York, New Jersey, and Connecticut. I initiated a program called the CSR three-step. CSR = Customer Service Representative.

Before signing on to a workstation, all of the employees were instructed to do the following three steps:

1. Clean the front doors
2. Clean all counters
3. Clean the workstation

This happened at the beginning of everyone's shift without fail, so all doors, counters, and workstations were cleaned at least five times a day. Good!

Even though it was a drop in the bucket with regard to the effort it took to grow the division from worst in the company to first place in sales, it was the definitive first step to growing the business. It is a foundation of the discipline that retail success demands.

Remember the blue pen you used a few pages ago? Take it out again and underline this next sentence. **All glass, metal, and counters should be sparkling, all of the time.** I don't care if the building is about to collapse, clean the damn windows. (You probably can tell that I feel somewhat strongly about this.)

The point is this: if Windex®, a paint brush, a hammer and nail, paper towels, a lawn mower, or a mop can make a difference, then use Action Step I, engage your motor skills and take a crucial step to drive your business.

Windex®,
a paint brush,
a hammer & nail,
a replaced light bulb
paper towels,
a lawn mower,
or a mop,
All help to make
A Difference

"No matter what your product or
service is, cleanliness counts."

Later in my career, a financial company that had many locations throughout the United States recruited me. This company had gone through a quick expansion process by converting everything from old gas stations, fast-food chains and defunct karate studios into retail loan centers. When I came on board, I tried to roll out a cleanliness program. It was met with great resistance and excuses. Eventually, with much prodding, the company or at least parts of it, grudgingly adopted a cleanliness program. And as predicted, the stores that sparkled had sparkling results.

These examples prove my point about the first "P"—**Place**—doing everything possible to control the atmosphere and ambiance of your workplace. Being aware and mindful of what your customer sees, looking at your place of business through their eyes. Incorporating measures to convey the best possible impression is the focus of the thinking and discipline that retail success demands.

Before we move on, there are two more must-mentions on what the customer sees: signage and colors.

Regarding signage, always maximize the space allotted. Get representation on the pole sign and put a sign up on every side of the building that can be seen from any street, but be tactful in this pursuit. In some businesses, I've been able to document that 50% of the customer base came strictly from a building's signage.

The Power of Signs. Check out the actual aggregate results of four different stores that opened under my watch. These four locations were located in the same geographical area.

Increase or Decrease in Customer Base

Unit A	33%	
Unit B	33%	
Unit C	-30%	(Sign removed)
Unit D	40%	

As I was responsible for the previously detailed expansion market, I was able to track the actual growth per unit as compared to the market. As you can see, all of the business units grew at 30% to 40%. The growth was for a two-week time period. Because of a local ordinance, I was forced to remove a pole sign for Unit C. The results were dismal; not only did the unit fail to grow new customers, it actually *lost* customers. There you have it, the power of signs.

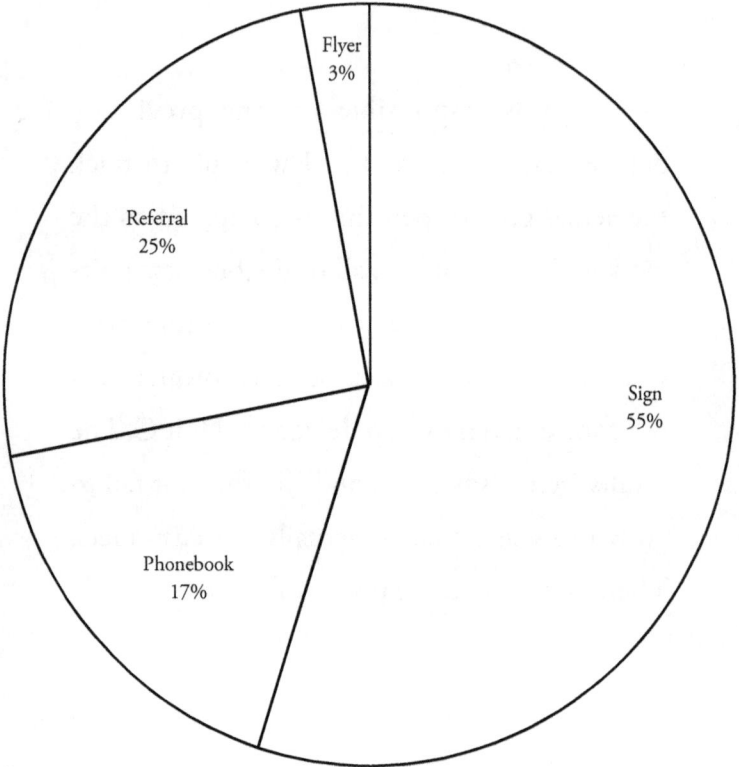

First 100 Customers

Flyer 3%

Referral 25%

Sign 55%

Phonebook 17%

The graph at the left is for yet another market that I was responsible for opening. It details how the first 100 customers responded to the question, "How'd you hear about us?" The graph says it all.

The Power of Colors. Numerous experts have explored the effects of colors and how they are interpreted. It's been proven that different colors have different meanings and tap into different emotions. Trust me, the most successful retailers spend a good deal of time pondering the matter of color—and those featured in their logos and sales materials weren't selected by chance.

To give you a general overview, I've cross-tabulated a few lists:

The Power of Colors

Color:	Meaning:
Black	Conservative & Sophisticated
Silver	Sleek & Glamorous
Brown	Earthy & Simple
Blue	Strong & Intelligent
Green	Growth & Health
Red	Passion & Joy
Pink	Romance & Playful
Yellow	Happy & Remembrance
Orange	Energy & Change
Purple	Royal & Precious

If you are in a position to create a new logo or color scheme for your business, please consider the list on the previous page and spend some time further researching colors. This list reflects the positive emotions elicited by colors, yet there is much more that you can explore. Read the list again. Can you see why some companies very specifically picked certain colors to represent them and their products? Think Victoria's Secret (red and pink) and Starbucks (brown and green).

One final point on colors, signage, and all that your potential customer *sees*. The simple fact is that black letters on a white background can be seen from a farther distance than any other color combination. This factoid comes from one of the many advertising classes I struggled through at the City University of New York, and it has served me well. Light your sign overnight with black lettering on a white background and it will be seen from the space station. All right, I'm exaggerating, but wow, that combination does glow! (By the way, did you notice the cover of this book?)

Smell. *What the customer smells.* More so than any of the other senses, smell serves as a recognition function. Smell and memory are intimately linked. Though this phenomenon is not completely understood, it doesn't mean that we can't use it to our advantage. Shouldn't every place offering health or dental care be and SMELL clean and every bakery have the aroma of freshly baked bread? But those are the easy ones.

Have you ever walked toward a restaurant but, on the way from the parking lot to the entrance, smelled rotting kitchen refuse? That couldn't have enticed your palate. Other smells that have affected personal shopping experiences: a clothing store reeking of a pesticide from the neighboring food establishment, a bank smelling like the grease of a fast-food place next door...and so on.

Incense, candles, cleanser, fresh flowers, cologne worn by employees, the hot-out-of-the-oven specialty—these are all ways to enhance the customer's experience.

Taste. *What the customer eats and drinks.* If you own or want to own a food establishment, use a quality product, seriously. Unless you are targeting a fast-food crowd, don't scrimp. Any sub-par products that save you money up front will hurt you in the end.

For non-food establishments: mints on the counter, fresh coffee, or donuts for your customers go a long way toward customer satisfaction. Some hotels provide freshly baked cookies for guests upon registration. Many car repair shops offer cold soda for waiting customers. It's an easy way to enhance the customer experience for a minimal amount of money. Another example: I flew on a Caribbean airline. The entire airline was coach class, yet as we took our seats, champagne was offered to all. That's 80 people enamored with an airline for the cost of two bottles of inexpensive Champagne.

Sound. *What the customer hears*. This is perhaps the easiest of all the senses to accommodate. Music adds atmosphere to every situation. Make it appropriate, play it always, and have speakers that play to the inside and outside of your establishment. A note on negative sound: employee banter should be kept to a minimum if the customer isn't engaged in it. It can be distracting or uncomfortable. On the other hand, there's nothing wrong with a jovial group of employees having fun with your customers or making them feel like part of the "family." And if you have talent on your team, why not use it? Many restaurants exploit this asset.

Touch. *What the customer touches.* You'd think this would be complicated, but it's an easy one. When anyone—prospects, existing customers, fellow employees, delivery drivers, neighboring store owners—enters your place of business, stand up, look them in the eye, greet them enthusiastically, and shake their hand. Every person. Every day. That, my friends, is powerful. Execute this with sincerity, and people will be just as excited to see you. By simply acknowledging each and every person walking through your door with a positive, cheerful greeting and a handshake, customer loyalty is born.

This concludes **Action Step I.** Good stuff, yes? To summarize, imagine a beautifully clear sign and spotless location, music greeting you as you walk up to a sparkling clean glass door, an enticing smell filling your lungs, and a firm, sincere handshake as you walk through the door. This is what it takes. This is the discipline.

PEOPLE

Action Step II. The next "P" stands for **PEOPLE**. You must choose the right people to represent you and/or your product, because the team you create to build your business is the most important asset you'll ever manage. Ever. Period. Read that again and underline it!

Now if we could only get the financial guys to understand the simple truth: numbers, spread sheets, and reports don't drive numbers, people do.

Numbers are simply the score card.

Before I give you some pointers that have worked for me, let me share some examples of people going above and beyond the call of duty—the type of people you'd like to have on your team.

The CEO at my last job got the order from on high (the shareholders) that we needed to expand rapidly in a particular state. Meaning, we needed to secure A+ retail sites before the competition infiltrated the market. We literally got on the next flight out, cancelled all personal obligations (of which there were many), and hit the ground running nonstop for 17 consecutive hours. Now *that's* dedication. Sites were secured and business ramp-up was remarkable.

During the holidays, as you'd imagine, the catering business gets very busy. Every Christmas, everybody pulled double shifts. That's what the business demands, yet somehow, I still miss the hospitality industry. Anyway, I remember one Christmas Eve when my shift started at five a.m. I worked through the breakfast and lunch rushes, and between the lines of demanding fast-paced New Yorkers, I assembled beautiful delicacies for orders that were placed in advance by well-planning, festive-minded customers. That evening, one of the night staffers didn't show up (or call), so I just kept slicing, dicing, creating, and assembling through the night. Five a.m. came around all too soon and customer pick-ups and deliveries started going out all over again. Thirty-one hours later, by noon, the walk-in refrigerator box was empty. I went home and slept for twelve hours—but I did what it took for the business to be successful, or I should say, for the customers to be satisfied.

I worked in the video rental business on two continents, for three different brands. As a rule, store inventories were conducted on a monthly basis; they all started at midnight, after close of business. Just to have a staff present was a lot to ask, let alone what a particular team accomplished in the Northeastern United States. Check out this dedication: we'd just completed an acquisition of two stores in Connecticut. The inventory was a total disaster for many reasons, one being that there were thousands of unaccounted for videos in a storage room that *escaped* being identified during the corporate office's due diligence process.

As store staffs completed their own inventories at about 6 a.m., they drove from New York and New Jersey to assist the manager and myself (I was a district manager at the time) at the Connecticut location. Now *that's* teamwork and dedication. Would you believe that one of the higher-ups questioned overtime hours? (Yes, I would. They don't work in the trenches.)

This discussion about overtime often leads to micromanagement tactics taken by upper management, or people that impose their wills and perspectives from the luxury of the sidelines. When you get to an upper-management position, before you jump to a conclusion and over-analyze a situation, ask your rank and file a few questions first. (There *is* a reason analysis and analyze both start with the word anal.) To get the kind of dedication from your team as I've illustrated with the above anecdotes, you need to manage by the "Power of Trust." Micromanagement will NEVER get your troops to march the extra mile. Never. Absolutely always inspect what you expect, but if you don't trust someone, they shouldn't be on your payroll. So be careful to judge and treat employees with dignity, fairness, and respect.

Judge
and treat
employees with
dignity,
fairness,
and respect

So how do you pick your team? Years ago, I read a quote in one of Og Mandino's books: *"Experience is like fashion, what worked yesterday does not work today."* That thought has stayed with me; so much so, that it is very rare that I hire employees from the industry I am recruiting for. First of all, outside candidates will not come in with their old company's spin on things and you can teach them your angle on the industry and your processes.

Secondly, and most importantly, I hire people that I can trust and that have unbridled enthusiasm. This, my friends, cannot be gleaned from perusing a resumé. Following is a sample of the questions I ask during an interview. I've had candidates complain about the process, and I've had my superiors question my process as well, but in the end and without fail, the teams of individuals I pick have always delivered above-standard results and place in the top rankings, month after month, industry after industry, time after time.

Creative Interview Questions

The following are among the non-traditional questions I like to ask candidates interviewing for positions at any level. Not only do these questions elicit information that often reveal a great deal about an individual, but the way the candidate reacts and delivers their response is very telling as well.

Creative Interview Questions

What's your favorite movie?

What's the last book you've read?

What are your three favorite books?

What was your very first job? How long did you stay? Why did you leave?

What's your favorite TV show?

Tell me about the last time you were late to work.

Has anyone ever made you feel uncomfortable?

If you could take the trip of a lifetime, where would you go?

Favorite meal?

If you could drive any car in the world, what would it be?

Favorite sport to watch?

Favorite to participate in?

Are you comfortable working with all types of people?

Hobbies?

Passions?

What are the three most important things in your life?

What have you done to enhance each of these three?

Favorite band or entertainer?

Favorite song?

Which section of the newspaper do you turn to first?

What's the best thing you've done for your fellow employees?

What are the top three attributes of a leader?

What public figure do you respect?

People
drive the
business,
not
numbers

I pay very close attention to body language and the timing of candidates' answers. If a person responds without much hesitation, or they're locked in sincere thought to find a true answer, you've got an honest candidate. And if you can't get a quick, sincere answer as to a candidate's favorite movie or TV show, there are other, deeper issues—trust me.

If they slouch and can't make regular eye contact, they are not interested. If they lean forward, they're very enthusiastic and enjoy the rhythm of the questioning. They'll probably like your style. That's a winner. The analytical types will be upset because you haven't asked about numbers or percentages—their own safety zone—but remember, when it comes to happy customers, People drive the business, not numbers! Quoting revenues at your last job isn't going to entice Stephanie to buy the product that you are trying to sell her today.

*"Smiles are contagious and
conducive to success"*

To wrap it up, hire those who are happy to be on your team. Recognize their efforts. Know that they do it for you and (and this is a big AND) give them the recognition AND time off they deserve. In the previous example about the overtime, this stuff actually happens. Corporate America blacks out months, days and weeks that employees can't take off. Instead, how about we let the people shedding blood, sweat, and tears for us—you know, making us successful—take *mandatory* days off? Some well-earned and recognized down time. Believe me, it goes a long way, and it has been earned. During a start-up phase in one of the expansion companies I was with, I'd make field management go see a movie midday, a two-hour sojourn to help clear their stressed minds. It's about creating an allegiance that can't be bought and is earned for all of the right reasons...

PARTNERS

Action Step III. *Create effective Business Partnerships.* **The last "P" stands for BUSINESS PARTNERS.** Strive to create and maintain relationships with other businesses that are mutually beneficial for all parties concerned, including the companies' customers.

Let me share an example of one of the best and most creative business partnerships I've ever been a part of. The costs were minimal and the results remarkable. The partnership was between a small personal loan business and a video store. Both businesses had multiple stores in the Carolinas. I was in the marketing department of the loan company, and in my martial arts program, I met the owner of a regional video chain. We quickly became friends and spoke shop because I had been in the video retail industry for a few years.

As we worked our way through the Karate curriculum, we discussed the industry challenges, including marketing and advertising costs and getting delinquent customers to pay on late or non-returned videos. Then we discussed the challenges of the loan business—they are the same! Marketing costs, the cost of new customer acquisition, and getting delinquent customers to pay us back on time was problematic for my company as well as his.

Interesting that we shared these common concerns in such different fields but when you think about it, these are universal challenges for all businesses.

One thing we both could offer each other was **exposure to each other's customer bases.** The second most valuable asset in business is your customer base (the first, for those of you suffering from short-term memory loss because of one too many concerts or parties or philosophy classes—is your employees.) So here's how we went about "exposing ourselves."

Signage

I hung one of my company's posters on my partner's new release wall—so as a customer you'd see all the new movies available to be rented and a poster for the loan company. In turn, I put a movie poster with my partner's logo in every one of the loan stores in the same territory.

Collecting on Late Paying Customers

To keep the loan customers extra-motivated to pay back on time, for every on-time payment we received we issued a rent one/get one free coupon for my partner's video stores. This drove down late payments. At my partner's stores, standard procedure was to send out late letters to his delinquent customers. He inserted the loan company's info in the mailing as a solution, or a way for his customers to get the money to pay him back. (At the time, new release rental videos were priced at $80+.)

More Exposure

All of the loan stores were issued pens for use with the video stores logo on them, and all the video stores were issued pens for use with the loan company's name and logo on them.

The loan stores bought plastic check-out bags for the video stores, but before giving them to the video stores, they'd stuff the bags with loan store flyers.

At customer-appreciation events (either company), balloons with printed logos were supplied for the partner's event.

Video stores would often have PVT sales (PVT = Previously Viewed Tapes). I let the video store set up a table in our loan store for a few hours during our busy period and ring up sales for themselves.

On busy weekend nights at the video store, the loan store was allowed to stuff their flyer into the videocassette boxes. A win-win situation for both companies. Both partners got their information distributed for free, the video company with their coupons being distributed at the loan company's counters, and the loan company by stuffing the check-out bags, videocassette holders, and late letters.

Both companies got their logos in front of a captivated customer base with the swapping of the posters. Both partners' employees had more fun during the exchange of information, the events, and the positive energy of the symbiotic relationship. (One more time: take care of your employees and make it fun, and they'll take care of your business.)

Take care of
your
employees
and make it fun,
and they'll
take care of
your
business

In summary, business partnerships mean your customers get an added value at no cost to you. Your partner gets exposure to your customer base at no cost to him. And your employees have another reason to be proud to work for you. Now that's a Slam Dunk!

Other Successful Partnerships

An ice-cream shop partnered with a delicatessen. Buy lunch at the delicatessen; get a free dessert coupon for the ice-cream shop. That added value for the deli's customers, and the deli enjoyed the credibility of being associated with Carvel, a national ice-cream chain. The ice-cream shop got exposure to the deli's customer base and free distribution of their coupons.

A Karate school partnered with a video store. The Karate school would perform demonstrations in or in front of the video store, taking names for their mailing lists and raffling off free lessons for a year. This added value for the video store's customers at no cost. The video store signed up all the Karate students under their "student discount" program and instantly expanded their customer base. There was some cross-merchandising as well. The Karate school set up a display in the video store and the video store set up a display of Martial Arts videos for sale in the Dojo. Again, a win-win situation that cost little to no money.

So how do you go about setting up these partnerships? The first rule is to Go to Who You Know. What industries, businesses, brands, or stores have you worked for or in? What clubs or associations do you or have you belonged to? What line of work are your friends and neighbors employed in? With whom do you share similar hobbies and interests? Think about this for a moment and list them on the following page. As more ideas come to you, come back to this section and expand your list.

Who I Know

_____

_____

_____

_____

_____

_____

_____

_____

_____

_____

_____

_____

_____

_____

As a standard approach to business partners, always use manners. If you're trying to hook up with a particular business, perhaps use their service first, then segue into a discussion about a partnership. Always send a thank-you note. Introduce yourself with the same enthusiasm that you would a customer when they enter your store. Consider your potential partner's busy times and do not approach them during it. Again, common courtesy and manners.

One final example that shows how easy it is to establish partnerships when you are "on" — thinking about and incorporating your business into day-to-day life 24/7. My Jeep dropped its transmission. Repair costs exceeded $3,000. I was aggravated and aggressive to say the least (I *am* from New York). The manager calmed me down, explained the problem, showed me the broken metal "thingys," and made me feel at least a little better about the project. As soon as I composed myself, I went right back into business mode and asked him how people were able to come up with that much money that quickly. I figured if he was able to calm me down and showed that much caring for his customers, I wanted to be associated with him. He said that if his customers didn't have the money, he'd fill out a loan application for them and fax it to a local bank, though, he said many loans are turned down, "But we do try."

Bingo! At the time I was in the loan business as well, and the stores I managed had much more lenient underwriting rules than banks. We set up a partnership that day! I had the manager from the nearest loan store make a visit to the transmission shop. The managers of both businesses were introduced to each other and a partnership blossomed.

Keep in mind that manners are a sign of respect for people, so always mind your manners. Here are five steps to building strong business partnerships:

1. Never talk shop when your potential partner is busy

2. Always send a thank you note

3. After the partnership is established, continue to visit your partner to keep your arrangement "top of mind"

4. Invite your partners to all customer-appreciation events

5. Recommend your partners to others

Manners

are a

sign of

respect

for

people

Another avenue to consider when forming a business partnership is to Go to Where Your Customers Goes. Where else, besides your store(s), does your customer shop? After you deduce that, get to know that business and link up as the opportunity presents itself. List these businesses on the following page. This might take some time and thought, but seriously—think about it. Who knows your customer better than you do? And finally, just ask them. Make it part of your casual conversations. "Where are you off to today?" or "Traffic looks rough, where'd you drive in from?" And so on...

Where My Customer Goes

_____

_____

_____

_____

_____

_____

_____

_____

_____

_____

_____

_____

_____

Lastly, get to know your neighbors. Every business located next to and across from your business should know your name, what you do, and what services you offer. Eventually, this should spread to your entire trade area. Everyone should say, "Oh yeah, that's Tommy from _____, he's got the best _____ in town". Or some derivative of that. List your business neighbors on the next page.

My Business Neighbors

_____

_____

_____

_____

_____

_____

_____

_____

_____

_____

_____

_____

_____

_____

_____

Whenever I'm consulted to visit and advise on a business, I always take a stroll through the neighborhood. This is a healthy exercise, as always, pun intended. On one such occasion, I walked into a Sarah Lee Bakery. In the food industry, sampling drives sales 600%. That means that if you let your potential customers sample your food product, they are *six times* more likely to buy it. I'm sure you've seen this in most food courts or supermarkets that you've frequented. Now you know why.

Back to the bakery. Sarah Lee was doing just that, handing out samples to everyone entering their store. I spoke with the manager and suggested that instead of just rewarding their existing customers who were already in the store, why not set up a station in the business I was representing? Another slam dunk. Sarah Lee handed out samples to my customer base as they waited on line, along with a coupon and a smile. They saw a significant increase in sales that day because they tapped in to my customer base. My customers felt special because they received a treat for free, and of course, the employees from both companies deemed it a huge success and planned to run the program once a month. Business Partners. Create the relationship, groom the relationship, execute the principles, and reap the benefits.

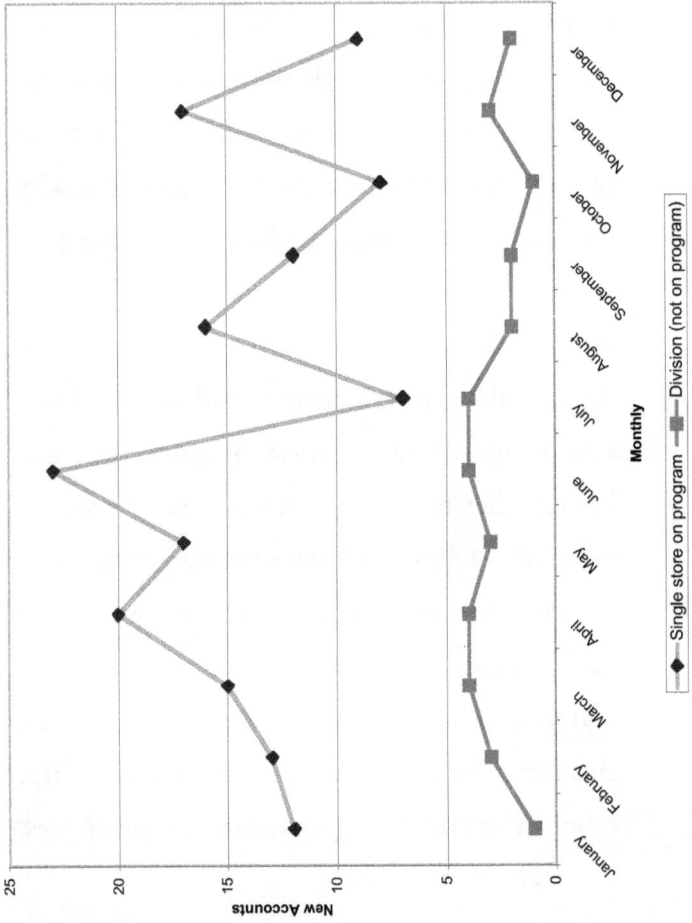

Average New Customers Per Month

New Accounts

25 — 20 — 15 — 10 — 5 — 0

January, February, March, April, May, June, July, August, September, October, November, December

Monthly

— Single store on program
— Division (not on program)

On the previous page, you'll find a graph that says it all. These are results for a company I worked with in the recent past. I rolled out the Trench Marketing Program in a store that was part of a region consisting of 25+ stores. Look at the difference! The store on the program increased their customer count by 81% over stores not on the program. Now that's irrefutable evidence.

Put on Your Shades, Your Future's Bright!

I **know that it sounds like I am slamming** traditional advertising and marketing, and the associated agencies, mostly because I am. That said, the people I've met at the agencies are truly the most gifted and educated that I've met in any industry. I just believe that it's time for a different approach.

After joining me on this journey of success in business, you'll probably refer back to this book the rest of your career. So to summarize one last time, keep your business pristine and welcoming by exciting all of the senses. Hire the right people and treat them exceptionally well because they're the most valuable asset you have. And create lasting business partnerships using common sense, manners, and follow-through. Do all of this, all of the time, and you can't help but succeed.

Know that luck favors action. Staring at a computer screen, continually reviewing reports, barking orders over a phone while remaining hidden in the ivory tower, creating manuals and memos—all of these exercises do not change behavior. Not in a good way anyway. I'm not saying reviewing results and implementing and creating standards of operation aren't necessary. What I'm saying is that it is necessary, but not the focus of business. Set a goal. Strategize how to get there with input from your team. Script the how-to and support materials you'll need to get there. And then, get out there and make a difference. Stand behind your counter and greet customers, seat customers, smile at customers, and get customers to smile back at you. That's what this is all about.

The final revelations are these, and I call them revelations because so few people seem to inherently know this.

Insist on enjoying life. You only get one shot at it. It *is* OK to smile at work. Smiles are contagious. If they seem not to be, change your scenery, quickly.

And above all, laugh. Relish the feeling. Laugh from within. Laugh with everything you have till it hurts.

I look forward to hearing about your successes!

Oh yeah, about the date. It ended up being another little blonde mistake that I was more than happy to make...

Rudy can be booked for lectures or consulting by emailing him at TrenchMarketer@aol.com or via his website at www.TrenchMarketer.com or www.Facebook.com/TrenchMarketer.

If you have a success story using Rudy's Trench Marketing principles, please share on the "Marketing from the Trenches" Facebook page.

Is your company in a rut? Drowning in social media, deliberating what the next-best-program is, struggling with diluted ad campaigns, etc.? Set them right by getting back to the basics. Buy a copy for everyone. Make a difference.

This book is available for bulk sale. To inquire about pricing of ten or more copies (sold at a dramatic discount, non-returnable) please email us at TrenchMarketer@aol.com.

Bibliography

Bibliography

Blanchard, Kenneth, and Spencer Johnson. The One Minute Manager. New York: Berkley Books, 1983.

Coelho, Paulo. The Alchemist. San Francisco: HarperSanFrancisco, 1998.

Gladwell, Malcolm. Blink. New York: Little, Brown and Company, 2005.

Godin, Seth. Permission Marketing. New York: Simon & Schuster, 1999.

Goldberg, Natalie. Wild Mind: Living the Writer's Life. New York: Bantam Books, 1990.

Hargrave, Jan. Let Me See Your Body Talk. Dubuque: Kendall/Hunt, 1996.

Hickman, Craig R. Mind of a Manager, Soul of a Leader. New York: John Wiley & Sons, Inc., 1992.

Levinson, Jay C. Guerilla Marketing Attack. Boston: Houghton Mifflin Company, 1989.

Mandino, Og. The Greatest Salesman in the World. New York: Bantam Books, 1974.

Mandino, Og. The Greatest Salesman in the World Part II. New York: Bantam Books, 1989.

Mandino, Og. The Greatest Secret in the World. Hollywood, Fl: Bantam Books, 1978.

Pearce, Terry. Leading Out Loud. San Francisco: Jossey-Bass, 1995.

Ries, Al, and Jack Trout. The 22 Immutable Laws of Marketing. 1st ed. New York: HarperBusiness, 1994.

Ruiz, Don M. The Four Agreements. San Rafael: Wisdom Books, 1997.

Schultz, Howard. Pour Your Heart Into It. New York: Hyperion, 1997.

Weiser, Alice, and Jan Hargrave. Judge the Jury. Dubuque: Kendall/Hunt, 2000.

www.ingramcontent.com/pod-product-compliance
Lightning Source LLC
Chambersburg PA
CBHW020209200326
41521CB00005BA/304